GOING
THROUGH THE
MOTIONS

Opening Yourself to God's
Possibilities

Linda Schott & Marty Dodson

Christian Communications
P.O. Box 150
Nashville, TN 37202

Published by Christian Communications
A division of the Gospel Advocate Co.
P.O. Box 150, Nashville, TN 37202

ISBN 0-89225-312-6

CONTENTS

1. Living on the Edge 7
2. Is Your God Too Small? 15
3. Who's in Charge Here? 21
4. The Quiet Zone 28
5. God Seekers 35
6. Prayer: What's in It for Me? 43
7. Prayer: Where Do I Start? 50
8. The Mystery Guest 57
9. The Bumps Are What You Climb On! .. 65
10. Take a Bite! I Dare You! 75
11. Looking Out for . . . #2? 83
12. It Runs in the Family! 90
13. A Friend in Need 98

PROLOGUE

As writers, we have had a dream that we hope will be fulfilled by you, the reader. Our dream is to help you get to know the God that has made such a difference in our lives. Our challenge for you is summed up in our title. We believe God calls you to clear your life of the empty motions you go through and fill it with the real meaning He offers you as a Christian. The Christian life isn't a dull and boring existence where everyone sits around listening to sermon tapes. The life God calls you to is one beyond your imagination! God is waiting to take you and use you in ways that He's never used anyone before! We've been amazed at what God has done with ordinary people like us. Accept the challenge. We dare you! Drop all of the things that have kept you from growing closer to God. Take that first step out into the unknown and ask God to show you the possibilities for your life as you stop going through the motions and start building your faith in God.

We Love You!

Marty Dodson
Linda Schott

1

LIVING ON THE EDGE

Dear God:

It's me again! I'm pretty discouraged tonight—about this thing called Christianity. The minister had a lesson today on baptism. I have to confess that I felt a little smug, thinking I didn't need the lesson. I'm already a Christian! But as he talked, my mind wandered to the day I was baptized.

It was Mother's Day, four years ago. My best friend became a Christian that day, too. Everyone was so proud of me, and I was really excited and fired up for you!

What happened, Lord?

It's just not what I thought it was going to be. I go to church regularly, but there's something I don't understand. I keep hearing talk about "growth." I sure don't feel like I've grown any. In fact, I don't feel any different than I did the day I was baptized!

Sometimes at church I just feel like I'm in another class at school! And you know how B-O-R-I-N-G that can be!

I just don't seem to have my act together! I want my friends to see you in my life, but that's hard to do because I don't FEEL you in my life!

I guess what I'm trying to say, Lord, is that I'm tired of being a "nobody" in your kingdom. I want

my Christianity to stand for something. But how—
and what?

I want to be more like your Son. But how do I do
that?

Thanks for listening, God. You're always so quiet
when I talk to you.

Do you think you could help?

awsome letter

Jay

Have you, like Jay, asked yourself one or more of
these questions:

- How do I know God is real?
- Why is it so hard for me to pray?
- Why don't I enjoy Bible study more?
- Why don't I feel close to God when I worship?
- Is this all there is?

Everyone asks these questions. In finding the answers, sometimes it helps to . . .

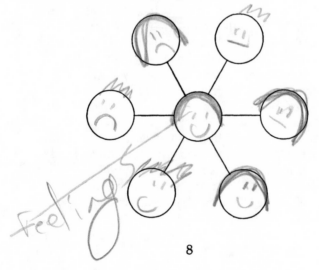

feelings

8

Go back to the very beginning. There are probably many people who influenced you to become a Christian. Put their names in these circles, but leave the center one blank.

Was there one person who seemed to be a "spiritual giant?" Put that person's name in the center circle. List three things that made you admire him in his daily life as a Christian.

1. _____

2. _____

3. _____

God knows just who to send us—at just the right time—to help us make the important decision to become a Christian. Think again about the day you were baptized . . .

At the time, it was an exhilarating experience. You knew you had done the right thing! But what did it REALLY mean? Was your baptism more than just a ritual that caused temporary happiness?

Take the time to write down some words that describe how you felt the day you were baptized.

_____, _____,

_____.

How did you feel (or how would you feel) about God forgiving all of your sins? _____

_____

_____

_____

_____

What changes occurred in your life after you were baptized? _____

_____

_____

_____

_____

Did your behavior, language, responsibility, or anything change?

☐ Yes   ☐ No

So what is this thing called baptism?

When you were buried with Christ in baptism, all of your sins were forgiven. That's called salvation. But being baptized and becoming a Christian means even more. It means that God is your partner for life! He will be with you always, and He will give you everything you need! His love for you is not based on your feelings. He knows that you can't always be on a spiritual "high." He will be there with you in the "lows" or the valleys, too!

Your Christian life won't stand still. Hopefully as you mature in years you will grow closer and closer to the Lord. Jay was concerned about this. He couldn't see any "growth." He wanted to become stronger in the Lord, to feel victorious—to love Christ more—but he didn't know how.

What do you think you need in order to grow spiritually? _____

_____

_____

Where are you on the growth chart? Do you see any great changes?

Try rating yourself on a scale of one to ten (with ten representing the highest and best) on the following statements. At the end of this study, we will

I haven't grown any...

Where are you on the growth chart?

look back at these ratings. Hopefully, you'll see a great improvement!

_____ 1. I spend time daily in prayer.

_____ 2. I like to attend Bible class and worship.

_____ 3. I study my Bible regularly.

_____ 4. I attend retreats, devotionals, etc.

_____ 5. My friends can tell from my conversation and activities that I am a Christian.

_____ 6. Jesus Christ is a very close, personal friend.

_____ 7. I make an effort to reach those who don't know the Lord or those who are spiritually weak.

_____ 8. I put God and Christianity before everything else.

_____ 9. I go out of my way to help others who are less fortunate than myself.

_____ 10. I am satisfied with my Christian walk.

What do these statements reveal? Are you discouraged? If that's so, you are sharing this feeling with thousands of teens across the country! And don't make the mistake of thinking adults can breeze into this "growth" with no problems! They, too, share your concern about their walk with Jesus Christ.

That's because Satan loves to put stumbling blocks on the path to spiritual growth, whether you're 15 or 55!

Do you have a stumbling block? Put a check mark below if you're . . .

_____ not as close to God as you would like to be;
_____ involved with some people who keep you away from God;
_____ looking for a "spiritual experience;"
_____ on a spiritual roller coaster, up one day and down the next;
_____ almost ready to call it quits.

Don't give up! It isn't always easy to be a Christian. If you've ever wondered what it takes to put all the pieces together, keep reading. It's all a part of disciplining yourself—and that's what this study is all about.

It's for you if you want to reach below the surface and come to know Jesus as a close, personal friend.

Hosea wrote a beautiful prayer in Hosea 6:3: "Oh that we might know the Lord! Let us press on to know Him, and He will respond to us as surely as the coming of dawn."

Put on your walking shoes...and open the door to a "new life in Christ Jesus!"

If you really want to know the Lord, He will respond!

Are you ready to begin the journey? Are you ready to grow spiritually? Then put on your walking shoes . . . and open the door to a "new life in Christ Jesus!"

Group Activities

For this activity you will need paper, pencils, and envelope. Try to imagine what kind of letter God would write if He were writing specifically to you to invite you to become His child. Be very personal as you write and be sure to include things that He would praise you for AND things that He might say you needed to change. You will be asked to share with the class the general idea of your letter, but no one else will ever read it, so open up and let the good and the bad come out as you write. Then seal it in the envelope and give it to your teacher. You will open it during the last week of this study.

Group Activity

How would your life be different if you didn't know the Lord? On the paper that has been placed on the wall, illustrate the sentence, "What a difference He's made in my life."

Illustrate some times that being a Christian should make a difference in your life.

Discussion

Discuss with your class members one or more of the following questions:

1. Think about beginnings. What does God expect of new Christians?

2. How are new Christians like babies?

3. Do Christians make a mistake in believing that their closeness to the Lord depends upon "feeling?"

IS YOUR GOD TOO SMALL?

Once a child was asked to draw His idea of God. He drew an elaborate picture of an old gentleman with a long, flowing beard, seated on a throne. Around him were many switches, each one labeled with names such as "thunder," "lightning," "rain," etc. God's long arm was stretched out, and He was saying, "Which switch shall I pull today?"

Write down the first five words you think of when you hear the word "God."

1. _almighty_   3. _great_   5. _powerful_
2. _strong_   4. _ruler_

What is your visual image of God? Several people, asked the same question, responded as follows:

"I see God in a long, white, flowing robe, but He's not a feeble old man. He's got brown hair and a beard and looks 35–40. He is a huge figure that stands just above the sky. At other times I picture Him sitting on a huge throne in a colossal throne room, and I am walking up to the throne to talk to Him. In both instances, He is loving and understanding, but I always know that His word is the last word. He seems very real when I'm out in a beautiful place in nature . . ."

What is your visual image of God?

"I picture God as a very, very big man almost like a giant. There are a lot of clouds everywhere. He has a very long white beard with piercing eyes, and there are little angels everywhere with harps. He sits in a seat that looks like a judge's seat in a courtroom. He has a very big book on His desk with a big feather pen."

"I see a vague figure of God with His raiment of white flowing with the breeze. As I talk, the angels listen compassionately. When I've asked for forgiveness, shouts of glory rise from heaven . . ."

"I picture God sitting in a field of green grass with a stream running through it and a bunch of animals sitting down by Him listening."

"God is everywhere I look. In trees, mountains, streams, and the sky. He is a bright light that always smiles . . .

There is a common thread running through most people's concept of God. The words "warm," "gentle," and "compassionate" are often used to describe God.

Think about this. Is your image of God the same as it was five years ago, or do you need a better way to communicate your ideas about Him and to Him? Does He seem close, or too far away to really be your friend? Maybe you've felt like Lisa . . .

"God . . . at times I feel like you're so far away. I imagine what it would be like to really see you face to face. Even when I was a little child, I used to pray that you would come to me, maybe in the dark of the night, and reveal yourself. I never could understand why you wouldn't! But even in my longing to see you, I still get confused about just who you are and what place you have in my life. I want so much to get to know you better! Will you help me?"

Lisa

What is God really like? Have you ever had a friend who was patient, kind, humble, unselfish, truthful, protective and trusting? It's hard to find a friend like that! But our God has each of these qualities! Isn't it exciting to have such a friend?!

Look up the following Scriptures and fill in the

blanks with a word or phrase from each passage that describes God:

Isaiah 5:16: _holy_

Isaiah 6:3: _holy_

Roman 6:23: _gift of God is eternal life_

1 Corinthians 13: _love never fails_

John 3:16: _God loved the world_

Below are the last words written by King David before His death. Underline each word that describes God.

"Blessed be thou, Lord God of Israel our Father, for ever and ever. Thine O Lord, is the greatness, and the power, and the glory, and the victory, and the majesty: for all that is in the heaven and in the earth is thine; thine is the kingdom, O lord, and thou art exalted as head above all. Both riches and honor come of thee, and thou reignest over all, and in thine hand is power and might; and in thine hand it is to make great, and to give strength to all (1 Chron. 29:10–13).

After reading these verses, read the story of the creation in Genesis 1. How do you develop a relationship with a God who is so powerful? It's easy for people to say that you should get to know God, but how do you really get to know someone whom you can't see, or hear, or touch?

Who is your best friend? ~~Adam M.~~ _? Johnny_

Discuss with the class some things you do when you are trying to get to know someone better and become friends.

Friendship usually begins with a casual meeting—maybe in a class at school, or a ballgame. You might have hit it off right away, or maybe you just felt a pulling toward that person. The next time you met, you carried on a conversation. You discovered that you had some things in common. As you came to know this friend, more and more you began to trust him. It was fun sharing secrets! Your love grew into a commitment, and you wanted to show that love by doing special things for him.

Through the years your relationship with God grew.

Now think about God. Your parents probably introduced you to Him at an early age. Through the years your relationship grew. You felt close to Him in nature, in your prayers, and in relationships with those you loved. Your commitment to Him grew as you saw what He had done for you, and you sealed your commitment with the act of baptism. The relationship is still growing, and it will continue to grow throughout your life. He will never move away. He will never leave you for someone else who might be prettier, or who might have more money and a faster car!

In the coming lessons, we're going to try to get to know this God-friend better. Meanwhile, try to spend some time with Him. He wants you to keep in touch so the two of you can keep building a stronger relationship even though you are separated for a while. Let a special part of your time this week be dedicated to getting to know God better. Just think what it will be like when you get to be with your close friend God in heaven forever!

Group Activities

Using old magazines, scissors, markers, pens, glue, and butcher paper, make a collage showing ways that God makes Himself known to you. You may cut out pictures, words, or anything else that represents ways that you know God. When you get through, be prepared to share your collage with the class and describe to them what the pictures represent.

For a second activity, divide into small groups. Take five or ten minutes to come up with a good definition of God. What is He? What does He do? When you come back together, share your ideas.

3

WHO'S IN CHARGE HERE?

Isn't it cozy to sit in front of a blazing fireplace on a cold winter evening? It has a soothing, hypnotic effect. But in just a matter of hours, the fire is reduced to nothing but dead, gray ashes. No light, no smoke, no heat. But watch out—at the bottom, under the cold embers, are a few hot coals, capable of starting a brand new fire!

The Christian life is like that. At times we feel cold, without life. Nothing seems to go right. Love for God is crowded out by the busy schedules we keep. That's when the flame goes out—when we ask, "Is this all there is?"

But the fire hasn't really been put out—it's just been buried beneath tons of clutter known as daily living! Hidden deep inside each of us is a secret ember, ready to be raised to a flame. God is still there, waiting to be placed again at the center of our life—where He belongs!

That's what discipline is all about. You probably don't like that word. It might remind you of the times you got a spanking, were grounded, or were punished in some other way. What's the worst punishment you remember from your early childhood? _____

_____

_____

There's another kind of discipline. It also hurts. And just like the other, it always pays off in the end. Webster defines it as "training that develops self-control, character, or orderliness and efficiency." It isn't surprising to learn that it comes from the word "disciple." To be a true disciple of Christ, we have to practice discipline. And because we are disciplining ourselves rather than someone else, we will refer to it as self-discipline.

If you've ever seen a karate demonstration, you have seen a great example of physical self-discipline. The karate expert who can break a concrete block uses every ounce of energy that his body can pull together. If he has properly trained his body to work as one unit, he will succeed in breaking the block. It is much the same with spiritual self-discipline. You can do great things as a Christian if you will discipline yourself each day to study the Bible, pray, and spend some time with God.

Paul talks about discipline in Galatians 6:9. Look up this verse and write its meaning in your own words in the spaces below.

And let us not grow weary while doing good, for in due season we shall reap if we do not lose heart.

_____

_____

Maybe I don't need this thing called self-discipline. Do you want to . . .

- reach below the surface and come to know Jesus Christ as a close, personal friend?
- turn your Christianity into a something that makes a difference in other people's lives?
- develop spiritual habits that will last a life-time?
- re-light the fire that has been snuffed out?

If you answered yes to any of the above, then you're ready to stop living a superficial Christian life. You're ready to become a disciplined person, changing and growing each day. You're ready to do more than just plod your way through each day, merely existing in a simple daze.

Christianity should make a difference. The world is starving for changed people—people who go below the surface. Have you ever met a person you instantly liked—but later found him to be very shallow? All he could talk about were dates and

Some people you instantly liked when you met turn out to be very shallow.

fast cars. Your opinion of him suddenly changed. Perhaps you sensed a lack of maturity—of caring for the really important things of life.

If we don't develop self-discipline, we will become just like that shallow person. We will go to church every Sunday—or maybe even more often. But something will be missing. We don't want to leave our Christianity on the church pew every Sunday morning—curled up like a shedded snake skin— and slip it back on at the next worship service! We want our Christianity to make a difference in everything we do!

In what other ways can discipline help me? Chances are if you are not disciplined in your Christian life, you will not be disciplined in other areas. For example, do you remember the time you were going to try to stop eating candy bars and cokes? Or the term paper you were going to begin early—and finish early? And the many times you were determined to study your Bible regularly?

Name some other projects which you started but never finished:

_____

_____

_____

_____

There's a Bible verse that might help during those weak moments when self-discipline is missing: "Let us not lose heart . . . for in due time we shall reap if we do not grow weary" (Gal. 6:9).

O.K. I realize I need to be more disciplined. How do I do it?

1. *Plan your life!* A disciplined life is a life that is planned! How do you spend your time? Record the average amount of time you spend in a normal day doing the following activities:

How do you spend your time?

6hr classes at school   ____ talking on phone
____ television   ____ radio
____ sleeping   ____ a job
____ Bible study   ____ time with friends
____ time with family   ____ sleeping
____ school activities   ____ service projects
____ homework   ✓ other

After you have finished, go back and place another number in front of each blank—showing which activities you feel should be top priority. Number one would be the most important.

Which activities do you think are taking up too much time?

school chores

Which activities would you be willing to cut back on so that you might have more time for Christian priorities? _____

2. *Make a schedule.* Fill in the following schedule. (Draw an hourly schedule—from 6:00 a.m. to 10:00 p.m. Sunday to Sunday.) First, fill in all the necessary times for school, sleep, work, eating, etc. Then, begin placing in your schedule the things you need to be doing as a self-disciplined Christian (for example, Bible study, prayer, etc.). Be sure to set aside some time for helping and ministering to others.

Now include all your extra-curricular activities. Some of these might have to be eliminated if they don't fall into the four priority activities mentioned earlier. Your day will only stretch so far. You can't do everything!

A balanced schedule is one which includes activities in these areas:

1. A quiet time with God

2. A time for ministering to others
3. Time for worship services and fellowship
4. Time for extra-curricular activities
5. Time for relaxation and recreation.

Analyze your schedule. Does it include all of these areas? You're on the road to becoming a self-disciplined Christian young person! And establishing the habits of good planning will carry you through many years that lie ahead.

You're really in a race. The runner must have a lot of self-discipline to get himself in shape. He must exercise diligently, warm up before the race, and give it everything he has. At the end, whether he wins or loses, he looks back and asks himself, "Is there anything I could have done better?"

At the end of each day, try to spend some time looking at the kind of race you ran. Did you do a good job trying to let God control your life today? Was your schedule acceptable? Did you waste a lot of time on unimportant things? Are there some mistakes you made that you could learn from?

Can you say, like Paul, "I have fought a good fight, I have finished my course, I have kept the faith" (2 Tim. 4:7).

Group Activity

A person with discipline sticks to a project. Pick something which you need to do but don't like to do. Make it your goal for the week to finish that project. Report to the class on your progress at the next meeting.

4

THE QUIET ZONE

Would you like to take all your school books and dump them into the Atlantic Ocean? Do you dream of sunny beaches in Florida? Are you easily irritated? Having trouble sleeping? Are you forgetful? Are your classes at school and church a real B-O-R-E?

If you answered "Yes" to more than two of the above, then you probably have the "hurry sickness." It can grab you by the throat and spin you around so fast you won't even notice the days passing by!

Escaping to a sunny beach every day isn't realistic. You are probably in need of what is commonly referred to as "quiet time." The dictionary calls it "solitude."

Deep inside every person is a longing for a quiet, reflective type of life. Try to imagine that the place deep within you is like the rooms in a large old attic, filled with broken dreams, frustrations, anger, heartbreak, and lost friendships. Now imagine that you can take a broom, sweep out the clutter, and make room for the things that really matter, such as time with God.

Hurry Sickness

A Soundproofed Life! Your favorite rock star probably records in a studio designed to keep out annoying noises. That's exactly what you have to do to your life—soundproof it! You have to find a very special place where you won't be disturbed . . . far away from the clatter of daily living. And that takes self-discipline! It's something that has to be planned—and practiced.

The Strength of Solitude. The Bible gives us many examples of great heroes who practiced solitude. There was Joshua, who feared he was going to lose a battle. He stood alone to pray and won a victory over five kings!

And then there was Elijah—he had problems

29

convincing Ahab that the Lord was God. He spent some time alone with God, and God sent fire from heaven to convince Ahab!

God had to do something a little more drastic to get Jonah to spend some time alone with Him. All those hours alone in the belly of a whale gave Jonah enough strength to preach to the people in Nineveh.

Where can you go to get away from everything and spend some time with God? Would God have to do something so drastic as to place you in the belly of a fish? List below several places you might be able to use for an occasional quiet time with God.

your room
outside
your closet

Wherever you choose, it must fit these requirements:
1. It must be out of the path of traffic.
2. It must be a place you can use in both good and bad weather.
3. It must be well-lighted.
4. It must be quiet!
Can you think of some other requirements?

Jesus Gave Us the Example. Over and over in the Bible we are told of times when Jesus left the crowd and went to be alone with God. He began his day in

30

prayer. Read Mark 1:35. What does it tell you about our Lord's quiet time?

_____

_____

_____

In His experience recorded in Luke 6:12, when did Jesus spend time alone with his Father?

_____at night_____

_____

_____

His disciples often went with Him on Jesus' journeys into quietness. Each time they grew a little.

You're probably saying . . . "But there's no time for quiet time. There's football practice, softball games, trips, parties, and dates."

What are some activities or circumstances that keep you from having a quiet time?

_____baseball games_____

_____

_____

It does take effort to find a place for God in the middle of these activities.

Plan of Attack

1. Earlier in the lesson we learned to have a special place to spend time with God. Again we learn that Jesus set the example: "Go into your inner room, and when you have shut your door, pray to your Father who is in secret, and your Father who sees you in secret will repay you" (Matt. 6:6, NASB).

2. Take "minute" breaks of quiet time. Spaced out through the day are tiny bits of time with no

one else around. During those precious moments, just think about God. Praise Him for the day. Think about all the things you are thankful for.

3. Enjoy nature. All of God's gifts of nature are given to us to enjoy. They are God's handiwork. As strange as it may seem, you should make friends with the animals, the birds, and the trees. If you love God's creation, you learn from it. Open your eyes! Wake up your senses! Celebrate life!

4. Enjoy special "one of a kind" moments. These are special times, when the first snow of the season falls . . . or the darkened sky on a clear evening under a blanket of stars . . . or while you enjoy the first rays of the spring sunshine. All are reasons to celebrate, take a deep breath, and thank God.

5. Set aside a special time. Think about your daily schedule. Set time on the clock which would be the best time for you to be quiet with God. Try to let nothing come between you and this special time. David, in Psalm 5:3, said, "My voice thou shalt hear in the _morning_: in the _morning_ will I direct my prayer unto thee."

5. Have all the necessary equipment—your Bible, a pencil, and maybe a song book, plus a notebook for recording your special thoughts and feelings. Spend some time reading a devotional book or magazine, such as TEENAGE CHRISTIAN. Then read from your Bible, trying to relate what you read to your everyday life. Spend some time just listening to your own thoughts and communing

Set aside a special time.

with God in prayer. Seek the quietness of His presence.

Only in silence can we let go and let God have control. As you rest quietly in God, make your prayer requests known to Him. Ask in quiet confidence. Ask Him to use your life for His purposes. Give Him your body, mind, and spirit. Tell Him of your imperfections. Let go of the demands of living that clutter your days.

If you've ever been canoeing, you know that usu-

33

ally after a period of rough, treacherous water, there is a quiet, still pool. It is the same in life. By partaking of a quiet time with the Lord, you can drink of still, quiet waters.

Group Activities

Divide into groups. Discuss what three things you would take with you if you were going to be alone on an island and wanted to continue your quiet time with God.

Discussion Questions

1. Suppose a person really hates getting up earlier, but this is the only time he can fit in a quiet time. Will the time be meaningful to that person?

2. Will every quiet time provide a "high" in Jesus?

3. What should be our chief motivation for a quiet time?

4. Discuss the following reasons for a quiet time:

• Spiritual cleansing
• Fellowship
• Goal-setting
• To become more like Christ.

5

GOD SEEKERS

God, I know you want me to study. But study is
all I ever do! I have to read books every day for
school. But yours is the hardest to understand. I
guess you probably wrote it for adults. I see the
words on the pages, but they sure don't excite me.
They don't seem practical. They're dry—just like
the dirt in the plants my mom forgets to water. I'm
sorry, God—I'm just being honest! You're going to
have to help me. Put a deep desire in me to study
your Word. Freshen up my Bible study. Talk to me
through your Word.

Sheri

Is God's Word getting top priority in your life? Chances are you don't see the value of spending a lot of time in God's Word at this stage in your life. You may think you're too busy, or it may seem too hard to understand. You might feel that Bible reading doesn't benefit you in any way. It's easy to see what consequences come from reading your English homework (or NOT reading it as the case may be!) But it seems that things go no better or no worse if you do or don't read your Bible. If you've ever had these feelings, really put yourself into this lesson. Give the Bible another try!

Have you ever heard of Steve Davis? He was a star quarterback at Oklahoma University for three years. In those years his team lost only one game. Steve was known as the guy with a football in one hand and a Bible in the other. He read His Bible every day and memorized hundreds of verses. In talks with others, he emphasized the importance of Bible study over and over. He seemed to be able to handle those passages that make us want to close up the Bible and go on to something more exciting. He probably had dry times, too. But he seemed to find a purpose and satisfaction in it all.

Perhaps he felt like the Psalmist who wrote the words in Psalm 1. "But his delight is in the law of the Lord and on His law he meditates days and nights."

The law the Psalmist is speaking of here is the Bible—God's word. To "meditate" means to think, ponder, or study.

What does this famous Psalm say will happen to

Just as the weight lifter develops muscles through training, we become strong spiritually through spiritual exercise.

a person who meditates on God's word? _____
_____
_____
_____

What did Job say of God's word in Job 23:12?
_____
_____
_____

Put 2 Peter 1:2–4 in your own words. _____
_____
_____
_____

What do you think God had in mind when He gave us the Bible? _____
_____
_____

What did He hope we would do with it? _____

_____

_____

_____

As you have already discovered, in order to be spiritually fit, there are certain disciplines that we must live by. Just as the weight lifter develops muscles through training, we become strong spiritually through spiritual exercises. Read what Paul had to say in 1 Timothy 4:8:

> For physical training is of some value, but godliness has value for all things, holding promise for both the present life and the life to come.

The first step in spiritual training is the Word of God.

The first step in spiritual training is the Word of God. Paul, in 1 Peter 2:2 wrote, "Like newborn babes, crave pure spiritual milk, so that by it you may grow up in your salvation."

That pure "spiritual" milk is contained in the Word of God. Think about it. Have you read any other book that:

- took 2000 years to write
- was written in three different languages
- on three continents
- by 37 authors
- with 66 parts

This book is one of a kind! Where else can you read about:

- animals that talk (Balaam and his donkey (Numbers 22)
- a man that is swallowed by a huge fish (Jonah)
- love poems (Song of Solomon)
- a miraculous escape from a fiery furnace (Daniel 3)
- a hand that appears at a banquet and writes on the wall (Daniel 5)
- a man who puts another man's ear on after it has been chopped off! (Luke 22)

In this amazing book is the world's greatest formula for success!

Read Hebrews 4:12 and write it in your own words. _____

By now you should be convinced of the importance of Bible study. Most people are! But getting down to the serious business of self-disciplined Bible study is another lesson in itself!

Make a Plan of Action!

1. Instead of trying to read the Bible through in one year, set smaller goals . . . perhaps one chapter from the Psalms and one chapter from Proverbs each day. Or you might read a major book through over a period of time, or read through a smaller book every day for several weeks. Included in your plan must be a specific time and a specific place to study God's word. Don't let anything come between you and your plan.

2. Ask questions. Is there anything in this passage that speaks directly to me? Is there an example for me to follow? A sin for me to forsake? A promise to claim? A new thought? What does it tell me about myself? What does it tell me about God? What does it tell me to do?

3. Use your imagination! As you read, try to place yourself in the situation. Try to imagine the scene. Close your eyes and see life as it was in Bible times. Can you see the winding Jordan River? At the baptism of Jesus, can you hear the gentle flapping wings of the dove as it landed on the shoulder of Jesus? The Bible says that the "heavens were opened." Look up and try to imagine what the peo-

ple saw that day. Listen to the booming voice of God when He said, "This is my beloved son, in whom I as well pleased." Sense the power and majesty of the moment.

4. Pray before you begin. Ask God to open your heart and mind to His direction. Ask Him to give you the message He is trying to speak through the printed page.

5. Write the verses in your own words. A special notebook will be helpful for this. Better known as paraphrasing, this is a simple method of making any difficult passage easier to understand. Sometimes a children's version of the Bible can help you through such passages.

Life will change when you abide in the Word and personally apply what it means in your life. Great blessings will be yours. That's a promise. "If you remain in me, and my words in you, ask whatever you wish, and it will be given you" John 15:7.

Group Activity

Form groups of five to eight people and have each group pick a parable and do a modern-day roleplay for the rest of the class. The skits need not be long or detailed. Try for creativity and getting the message across. Give a prize for the best skit!

Your first homework assignment! Memorize a passage of scripture longer than five verses. Try to choose one that is exciting and useful today. Your teacher should give you some verses to choose from.

GOING THROUGH THE MOTIONS

Take a few moments at the beginning of the next class to share what you have memorized.

Discussion

Read Deuteronomy 6:4–12. What do these verses teach about God and the importance of His word?

6

PRAYER: WHAT'S IN IT FOR ME?

God,

   I don't think you heard my prayer today. I want to talk to you so much, but sometimes I feel like you aren't even listening. Other times, I feel like you are right beside me. How can I make *all* of my prayers meaningful?

   One night last week, I went outside and the stars were so bright that they lit up the sky. I looked up and I could almost see you looking down on me. I could *feel you there!* I spent some time talking to you and I went back inside feeling really good. Thanks for times like that. I wish my everyday, ordinary prayers could be like that. Please send more of those times, God.

Colin

GOING THROUGH THE MOTIONS

Prayer is one of the most important parts of a Christian's life; yet it is often overlooked or neglected. How many times have you heard things like, "Everybody calm down so we can pray before we leave" or "Ooops, we forgot to pray for our food; everybody stop where you are!"? Times like that can give us the wrong impression of prayer. We think it is something you have to do before you eat, sleep, or go on a trip. Prayer isn't a last-minute insurance policy against indigestion, death in your sleep, or wrecks on the highway. Prayer is a time for talking to God! In this lesson, we will look at prayer and all of the things it can do.

What's In It For Me? Prayer can do all kinds of things for you! Of course, you have to remember that prayer isn't something to be used selfishly. Let's look at some of the things genuine prayer can do for you!

1. *Prayer can help you fight off temptation.* You probably have a lot of pressure at school. People, even your friends, try to get you to do things that you know a Christian shouldn't do. It seems like temptation to do something wrong is always waiting right around the corner, ready to grab you. Take a look at 1 Corinthians 10:13:

No temptation has seized you except what is common to man. And God is faithful; He will not let you be tempted beyond what you can bear. But when you are tempted, He will also provide a way out so that you can stand up to it (NIV).

Satan trembles when he sees the weakest saint on his knees.

There is an old saying that "Satan trembles when he sees the weakest saint on his knees." We can let God know about our temptations. Remember, Jesus had to put up with temptation too.

Read Philippians 4:6–7. What do these verses have to say about what prayer can do for you?

_____

_____

_____

_____

2. *Prayer brings forgiveness when you mess up.* Did you know that God just wants you to ask and He will forgive you? There's no magic formula, and no punishment. He forgives you, period! Not only

does He forgive you—He forgets all about your sins. That's something to be grateful for! It's nice to know that God isn't keeping score. Most of us would have lot of points in the sins column and not quite as many in our good column. David wrote a beautiful prayer in Psalm 51:1–3. Look it up and see what his attitude was when he went to God for forgiveness. Would you describe his request as:

(1) Proud
(2) Humble
(3) Cocky
(4) Sincere
(5) Fake

David didn't demand anything of God, did he? You get the impression that he was extremely upset and feeling guilty about his sins. He was begging God to go easy on him. You've probably seen courtrooms on television where the defendant begs for an easy sentence. That's what David is doing. He knows that he deserves death, but he asks for forgiveness and mercy from God. God loves you! Give Him a chance to show it by asking for forgiveness!

3. *Prayer can make your life happier.* A life that includes God regularly through Bible study and prayer can't be touched by any other way of life. Don't let people kid you. There isn't happiness in drugs, alcohol, or sex. In fact, there isn't even real happiness in things that we consider to be good, such as sports, band, or friends. If you're looking for

happiness, you're on the wrong road if you look anywhere but up! God has promised to make us joyful and complete. Take a look at John 16:23–24. Do you think this verse means that we will never have any bad things and that God will give us everything we ask for? Write down your own summary of the verses. _____

_____

_____

_____

_____

_____

_____

God has given you a direct phone line to Him, and it's up to you to make the calls.

God has given you a direct phone line to Him, but it's up to you to make the calls. Can you imagine having a direct phone to the President of the United States? Think of all that you could do if you had that much power! Wouldn't it be dumb to have something like that and never use it? Then why don't we pray more! You've got all the power in the world, even the power that made the world available to you in prayer. God can change your life if you will let Him. If it seems like you've been getting a busy signal when you call God, don't give up. God is listening. Use that power to make your world a better place!!

Group Activity

Grab two or three other people from your class and pull your chairs into a circle. Each of you should read Matthew 6:1–15. Then make a list of prayer "do's and don'ts". What should we use prayer for and what should we avoid? When you have finished, share your answers with the other groups. Then write your own prayer to God. Feel free to ask questions or to tell Him something new you learned about prayer. Try to use normal language, just like you would use if you were writing a friend.

Discussion

How often do you think Christians should pray?

- Once a day
- Constantly
- Morning and night
- At devotionals
- Before meals
- Other

If you asked around, you would probably get lots of different answers to this question! If you checked *constantly,* you are correct! Look up 1 Thessalonians 5:17. You are probably wondering how you are supposed to go to school and do all of the things you have to do if you are praying constantly. Actually, if you are doing what God says, your whole life will be a form of communication with Him.

Prayers don't have to start out "Dear God" and end with "Amen." They may consist of a simple "thanks" when things go good or "help" when you're in trouble. Discuss how you can live your prayers to God and write down your thoughts in these spaces. _____

_____

_____

_____

_____

_____

_____

_____

_____

_____

7

PRAYER: WHERE
DO I START?

> God is great;
> God is good;
> Let us thank Him
> For our food.
> Amen

You've probably heard kids pray. You may even remember some of the simple prayers that you said when you were younger. It's amazing how kids can say so much with just a few words! Sometimes it's funny to hear the things they pray for. One little boy, after asking his mother several questions on the subject, thanked God for giving him nose hairs to keep dirt out of his lungs! Another thanked Him for "doors" he could open! One of the things that kids have that we need in prayer is openness.

Remember to thank God for the things you are really thankful for, and let Him know what you think you need. Don't be afraid that your requests are too silly or unimportant for God to care about. He wants you to tell Him about the things that are going on in your life. If something is important to you, then it matters to God. In this lesson, we will look at the "School of Prayer" as we try to figure out the "how-to's" and the "how-not-to's" of praying.

1. *Be open to God's answer.* It may not be the answer you wanted, but be on the lookout for an answer to your prayers. It makes you wonder about the faith of people who come to the church building to pray for rain when no one brings an umbrella! If you are going to pray for something, expect an answer! Look up John 13:13–14 and rewrite it in your own words. *You should teach others about God, since God made and formed you.*

LORD, PLEASE LET ME PASS MY EXAMS!

You have got to do your part when you ask God for something.

Another thing to remember is that you must do your part when you ask God for something. A preacher was attending a luncheon, and the people

51

asked him to come forward and lead a special prayer for all of the hungry people in the world. To their surprise, he refused to do it! They were shocked and asked him why he wouldn't pray for hungry people. He answered that he didn't think God would appreciate their praying for something that they could do themselves. He then proceeded to walk around and asked each person to put their money in a hat. He collected almost $4,000. Only after they had done all they could for the hungry would he pray.

We ought to consider seriously what we have done about the things we pray for before we ask God's help. List some things that you pray for that you need to put some work into before you ask God to work on it:

help me to do well on my test
be with all the hungry people
help me to make good choices

2. *Make sure your heart is clean.* Read Psalm 66:18 and Matthew 5:23–24. How do you think God feels when we pray while we have sins we haven't confessed? *He listens to our prayers and feels great that we prayed, But is sad that we haven't confessed our sins*

We need to make sure our hearts are right when we make requests of God. If you have things you need to work out with the people around you, do something about them and go to God with a clean

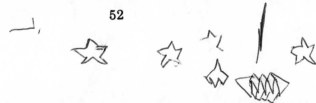

Confessing sins everyday is like taking a spiritual bath.

conscience. If you have sins you need to confess and ask God's forgiveness, do that first. Confessing our sins every day is like taking a spiritual bath. Do you think God wants us to say, "Please forgive me if I have sinned today," or does He want you to tell Him specifically what you did and what you plan to do to avoid that in the future? *he wants you to tell him what you did and how you're going to avoid it in the future*

You need to confess to God what you did. Don't give Him generic answers and explanations. He knows what you really did, so don't play around. It takes courage to say, "God, I had some lustful thoughts today and I cheated a little on my math test." But we should do it! It feels good to get the guilt off our chest and let God forgive us.

3. *Talk like you would to a friend.* Make a list of some words that you only hear in prayers at church.

fruit of the Spirit
In your name
ready recollection

Do you know what all of these words mean? You should talk to God like you would a friend. If you know what the big fancy words mean and want to use them to show respect to God, that's O.K. Don't use them just to sound impressive when you pray out loud at church. We shouldn't be any more showy in our public prayers than we are in our private talks with God. Read Luke 18:9–14 and write down what you think the verses are warning us against. _Don't be a hypocrite in_ _your prayers_

4. *Prayer particulars.* How many minutes per week would you say you spend praying to God? _20 min_ Do you plan times to pray or do you just pray when you feel a special need to? _both_ Where do you usually pray? _in my bed_ _or at the dinner table_

Ask the other people in your class or group how they answered the questions above. Then let's look at YOU again. If you don't plan special times to pray regularly, it's easy to fall into the trap of praying only when you need something from God. He wants your devotion all of the time. Have you ever had a "friend" who came around only when he wanted money or some special favor? That's how a lot of us treat God. We don't seem to care much about Him until we really need Him to get us out of some kind of mess.

Write down which five minutes of your days this week you could set aside to pray. _____ It could be early in the morning, at lunch time, or whenever works best for you. Give God those five minutes each day this week and then try to increase to ten minutes a day for the next week. Find a quiet place where you can be alone, read several Bible verses, and just talk to God.

5. *Prayer positions.* A lot of different prayer postures have been used through the years. Some people think that one way has special advantages, and others have their own ideas for prayer posture. Check the positions that you have used in prayer.

_____ Kneeling
_____ Standing
_____ Sitting
_____ Lying face down
_____ Looking toward heaven

Try out these different positions when you pray. Different positions might make different kinds of prayers more meaningful. Look up these verses and write down why praying in the position the Bible

55

describes might make the prayer more meaningful in certain situations:

Luke 22:41 _____

_____

2 Samuel 7:18 _____

_____

Mark 11:25 _____

_____

Ezekiel 3:23, 9:8 _____

_____

Which of the four positions mentioned in these verses might be most meaningful if you were

- Begging God to heal a deathly ill relative?
- Crying in repentance and confession of a sin
- Telling God what happened today and your feelings about it.
- Thanking God for all of your blessings?

Group Activity

Have everyone in your class pull their chairs into a circle. Pass a pencil with a writing pad around and let everyone write down things they would like the group to pray about. Select a person to read these prayer requests to God. Then allow time for everyone to add anything else they would like to pray about. Work on making the prayer conversational and personal. Don't pray for the *sick* in general; tell God WHO you are praying for who is sick and what you would like to see happen.

8

THE MYSTERY GUEST

The preacher talked today about the Holy Spirit. God, I tried to listen and understand, but I really have a lot of questions. How can you, Jesus, and the Spirit be one and the same? Is the Holy Spirit just a feeling? Is it real? Does He really live in my body? If so, how come I don't know He's there? Help me to understand, Lord. I am really curious about this Spirit. Do you think He might help me out? Thanks, God.

Mark

What can I know for sure about the Holy Spirit?

1. *The Holy Spirit is not imaginary!* He's not a vapor, or a phantom ghost like you see on Halloween. Jesus calls the Spirit "He" in John 16:8: "When HE comes HE will convict the world."

2. *He knows everything:* "For who among men knows the thoughts of a man except the man's spirit within him? In the same way, no one knows the thoughts of God except the Spirit of God" (1 Cor. 2:11).

3. *He is everywhere.* David, in Psalm 139:7–8 says, "Whither can I go from your Spirit? Where can I flee from your presence? If I go up to the heavens, you are there; if I make my bed in the depths, you are there."

4. *He is the third person of the trinity.* He is equal to God, the Father, and Jesus: "Therefore go and make disciples of all nations, baptizing them in the name of the Father, the Son, and the Holy Spirit" (Matt. 28:19).

Take a few minutes to write down what you know or feel about the Holy Spirit. _____

_____

_____

_____

_____

_____

_____

5. *Where is the Holy Spirit?* He is in your body! What does 1 Corinthians 6:19 say about this?

_____

_____

Isn't this thing called the Holy Spirit a great and exciting mystery?

The Holy Spirit dwells in you.

6. *What does the Holy Spirit do?* God gave the Spirit many responsibilities. Most important to you now is that He helps us to live like Christ. He has been sent by God, to us, to be our Guide. He accomplishes this by giving us a conscience, which in turn gives us the ability to overcome sin.

What temptations are causing you a lot of problems right now? _____
_____
_____
_____
_____
_____

Do you ever feel like there are two forces battling it out in your brain? One to do good, and the other evil?

The Spirit which lives in you, gives you the power to overcome temptation.

The Spirit, which lives in you, gives you the power to overcome temptation. He gives you the fruits of the Spirit, which are qualities you will bear if you live a Christ-centered life.

Look up these nine fruits in Galatians 5:22–23. List them in the spaces below. Beside each one place a number to rank it. Put a 1 beside the ones you're having the most trouble with; 10 beside those you have mastered.

_____

_____

_____

_____

_____

_____

_____

_____

_____

7. *What else does the Spirit do?* God has given us the Spirit to be our help and comfort in difficult times. Each day you face anxious moments and situations. Following are some stressful situations. Rank how you would cope with them, from 1–10, with 1 representing no anxiety and 10 high anxiety!

_____ breaking up with your boyfriend or girlfriend
_____ not getting accepted at the college of your choice.
_____ failing a very important exam
_____ a friend commits suicide
_____ your father loses his job
_____ problems with your parents
_____ America is plunged into another war
_____ your best friend betrays you
_____ a friend dies in a car accident

The Holy Spirit is God's gift to help you in such

times! Listen to these promises from the gospel of John:

> And I will ask the Father, and He will give you another Counselor to be with you forever.
>
> Peace I leave with you; my peace I give you . . . Do not let your hearts be troubled and do not be afraid.

Remember, these are the words of Jesus—a promise that He has sent the Spirit to give strength—to be with us in all things.

8. *The Holy Spirit is our honored guest.* When you have a visitor in your home, you go out of your way to make him or her comfortable. You honor his wishes and put your own possessions at his disposal. You don't shove your guest around, and you aren't rude to him. You do nothing to dishonor him.

Our very own personal honored guest is the Holy Spirit. Because He lives in us, there are certain things we can do that will dishonor and grieve Him.

Look up the following verses and write down what specific things grieve or hurt the Holy Spirit.

Ephesians 4:25: _____

Ephesians 4:26: _____

Ephesians 4:28: _____

Ephesians 5:3, 4: _____

Ephesians 4:31: _____

9. *Will having the Spirit cause me to feel anything special?* Walking in the Spirit, or the Spirit of Christ, does not cause lightning or thunder or powerful emotional feelings. It does make you

aware of a new ability to overcome sin, to be free from worry and stress, and to live a life of victory as a Christian. With the Holy Spirit in your life, you will be more sensitive to God and His plan for your life.

Even though the Spirit might still be a mystery to you because your understanding is limited, through the Scriptures you can know that the Holy Spirit, God, and Christ work so closely together that their thoughts are as one. It's an awesome thought—and one to be thankful for!

Write a prayer thanking God for the gift of the Holy Spirit.

_____

_____

_____

_____

_____

_____

_____

Group Activities

Tear or fold a sheet of paper or draw on it to demonstrate what the Holy Spirit does in the Christian's life. Remember the Scriptures studied in this lesson. Share what you create with the rest of the class.

To help you remember to work on the fruits of the spirit—especially those you are having difficulty with—write on an index card the name of each "fruit" that you scored below 5 on. Beneath the name of each fruit, write several things you want to try to do this week to improve in that area. For instance, if you are having trouble with joy, your card might look like this;

Joy

- I will smile more at school.
- I will thank God in my prayers for my blessings.
- I will write two people notes of encouragement.

Carry one card with you until you feel you have improved in that area. Then put this in a safe place and work on the next card. When you are finished, keep the cards. But carry one with you now and then to remind yourself of this great thing called the Holy Spirit!

9

THE BUMPS ARE WHAT YOU CLIMB ON

Dear God,

Last night Mom and Dad had another argument. It was the worst one yet. I don't know how much longer they will stay together. I used to think they loved each other. Boy, was I wrong!

I heard Mom talking about Mike. Lord, did you know that he took some money out of the register at work yesterday? Guess the boss fired him, because mom said there wouldn't be enough money to send him to college next year.

It was another bad day at school today. I just couldn't do anything right. At lunch Sally told me she likes another boy. I knew something was wrong, but I didn't know it was going to be THIS bad!

How much more, God. Things seemed to be going along so well, and then WHAM! It all hit at once. If one more thing happens, I might just go over the edge.

Are you going to help me, God?

Rick

GOING THROUGH THE MOTIONS

If you've ever found yourself asking God why so many bad things happen to you, you aren't alone! Everyone has times when they wonder why God couldn't go a littler easier! When you lose someone you love, or your parents get a divorce, or your best friend drops out of your life, it's a real drag.

Form groups of three or four people and answer the questions below as we look at ways we can grow when bad things happen.

Each person in the group should answer each question in turn:

1. One of the worst things that has ever happened to me is _____

_____

_____

2. When _____, who I was very close to, died, I felt _____

_____

_____

3. I feel _____ toward God when bad things happen.

4. I think God does/doesn't cause bad things to happen to me (Explain your answer.) _____

_____

_____

_____

Why do you think God lets bad things happen to good people?

_____

_____

_____

_____

Look up Isaiah 55:8. What does this verse say to you? _____

_____

_____

_____

_____

Thomas Wolfe, the great writer, said, "Man was born to live, to suffer, and to die—and whatever befalls him is a tragic lot. There is no denying this in the final end, but we must . . . we deny it all the way."

A pretty morbid picture, isn't it? But even though we would like to rebel against such an attitude, pain is part of life. If you had no pain, you would be only half alive. And who wants to take a detour around life?!

Pain is part of life.

Job, the great master of suffering, said, "Man that is born of woman is short of days and full of trouble."

John told us, "In this world ye shall have tribulation" (John 16:33).

Why does God allow suffering? It's the question of the ages. If we could sit down and talk to God today, it would probably be one of the first things we would ask Him.

There are some things we will never fully understand. There are some secret ways and thoughts that belong to God.

In Isaiah 55:8 we read: "For my _____ are not your _____, neither are your _____ my _____, saith the Lord."

A story was told of a parade passing down a very long street. The only way the spectators could view it was through knotholes in some fences along the way. They saw only parts of the parade. But God, in His wisdom and power, could see the whole parade from beginning to end.

So it is with life. Every bad situation threatens to destroy us. But God knows enough about us to see what we will need in order to be able to live with Him forever. He alone has the missing pieces of the puzzle. Our part is to trust Him and know that He will take care of us!

What does Romans 8:28 tell us about suffering?

_____

_____

_____

Do you really believe God can make good things come out of the horrible events of life? _____

In the space below, write down any good things you have seen come out of bad experiences in your own life.

_____

_____

_____

_____

_____

God wants you to lean on Him when things don't go well. If you think about it, your heaviest prayer time is when things are going bad. Maybe that's God's way of getting close to you when you stray away during good times.

What trials are you facing right now? _____

_____

_____

_____

Can anything good come out of them? What will your trials do for you?

1. *Trials will increase your trust in God.* It's easy to say, "I love you, God," when things are going your way. But what do you say when the walls are crumbling down? God says, "I want you to trust me in your times of trouble, so I can rescue you, and you can give me glory" (Ps. 50:15, TLB).

Just as a soldier who fights in a battle receives wounds that cause scars, so does life give us battle scars. After each physical or emotional wound, we pick up the pieces and start all over. Soon there's another trial that leaves another scar. After each scar your trust in God grows a little more, until at the end you reach the point of total reliance on God.

What does James 1:2–4 tell us about that state?

_____

_____

_____

_____

2. *Trials will cause you to have a strong character.* How does a weight lifter build up those "macho" muscles? It's certainly not through watching television! It takes sweat and hard work. That's how you build character.

Do you remember the story of the pearl? It begins its journey as a small speck of sand that irritates the system of the oyster. Secretions are let out across many years until the result is a beautiful, glistening pearl. What began as a trial to the oyster turned into a priceless treasure!

A goldsmith was once asked how long he kept his gold in the fire. He answered, "Until I can see my face in it."

God often keeps us in the fire until He can see His own face reflected in our life! Job spoke of the same thing: "But He knows the way that I take; when He has tried me I shall come forth as gold" (Job 23:10).

3. *Trials will help you be more sensitive to the needs of others.* How do we become strong? By weeping and self-pity? Certainly not—it's by help-

ing others. True happiness comes when we invest our self in someone else. God commands us to do just that: "Bear one another's burdens, and so fulfill the law" (Gal. 6:2).

What does Paul say about this in Romans 15:1?

_____

_____

_____

_____

Helping others has a healing effect. How often have you changed feelings of gloom into cheer by helping someone? Perhaps you only listened—or might have offered advice. Maybe you helped in some physical way. Whatever you did, you left the situation a little stronger—with your own problems seeming a little smaller.

The writer of Proverbs knew this when he wrote: "He who sings songs to a heavy heart is like one who takes off a garment on a cold day, and like vinegar on a wound."

4. *Trials make us long for a better place.* When everything's going our way, we would like to remain on planet earth forever! Heaven doesn't seem real. But after a night of weeping, we can read Revelation 21:4 with new zeal. What five things does the writer tell us will NOT be in heaven?

_____

_____

_____

_____

_____

So I understand I'm going to have trials. But how

am I supposed to act when the world's caving in?!

With joy. Come on, you say, you don't mean that I should be happy when my family splits up—when I fail a class—when my girlfriend breaks up with me.

What does James 1:2 say? "Count it all _____, my brethren when you encounter various trials.

When you are going through bad times,...you don't go around with a long, weepy face.

That simply means that when you are going through bad times, you don't go around with a long, weepy face. You praise God for the blessings you DO have, and trust in Him to work with you through the bad times.

With trust. Earlier we talked about trusting God

in bad times. Write Joshua 1:9 in your own words.

_____

_____

_____

_____

If others see you trusting God in a calamity, your example just might influence them to react in the same way through their own trials!

Be accepting. We can't walk around our trials. We can't jump over them. We can't crawl under them. We can't wave a magic wand and make them disappear! We just simply have to grit our teeth, stare them straight in the eye, tell ourselves that we WILL come out the winner, and then trust in God to do the rest.

An old man and his son went into the forest to cut wood for ax handles. The boy began to chop but his father stopped him because he was cutting down trees in the center of the forest.

"These trees will not do, my son, for they have been protected by one another. They will not make good ax handles. Go to the top of that big hill. Cut down the trees there. They have been exposed to bad weather and disease, so they are the strongest trees in the forest. They will make the strongest ax handles."

Remember the story about the parade. God could see it from beginning to end. He sees your life that way. He knows what is best for you. He knows you need a few bumps and bruises in order to become refined as pure gold!

Group Activity

Distribute paper and pencils to each person in the class. Have them make a list of the top ten things that they worry about and the top ten hopes or dreams they have for their future. Take time for everyone to share their top ten lists. As each idea is brought out, put it on the board in either the worry or dream column. Note how many times the same ideas are brought up. It really can help to realize that you aren't alone and that lots of other people have the same worries and dreams you have. Even if no one brought up YOUR worries, God is always there for you. Lots of times, we forget to pray about our worries until they really happen. Tell the students to take home their lists and pray about their worries and dreams. Putting everything in God's hands from the beginning is a lot better than waiting until things fall apart to ask for help. Get to know God now, when things are going O.K. and you won't have to look up His number when you have to make an emergency call!

10

TAKE A BITE!
I DARE YOU!

God,
   I really blew it today! I thought everything about my Christian life was going so well and then someone said something today at school and I got so mad that I lost control of my tongue. I said some of the "big" ones, Lord. I guess you already knew that, didn't you? My friends were really surprised, but no more than I was. I thought I had that problem under control, but lately things just haven't gone my way. Please help me control my tongue and my thoughts when I get angry. I need your help, because I can't seem to overcome it on my own.

                                                            Becky

Don't you sometimes wish that the devil would just lay off you for a while? Just when you think you have everything under control, he finds your weakest moment and zaps you! We are going to take a look at temptation in this lesson. We will discover some ways to fight back and some ways to grow stronger when we are tempted to do wrong. Can't you just see the devil's face when he realizes his temptation is pushing us closer to God!

Why do I want to sin so badly? That's a question all of us have probably asked at times. Why couldn't God have made us to want to do good? Have you ever seen a box with "Private, Do Not Open" written on the top? Isn't it tempting to peek inside to see what is so important? God wanted us to have a choice, to be able to follow Him or to go our own way. That way, He knows which ones of us really want to be His people.

Open your Bible and read Ephesians 6:12. Who does this verse say we are fighting against? _____

_____

_____

_____

We are tempted in three ways. If you break all of our temptations down into basic categories, you find they will fit into three groups. Let's take a look at the groups and see how we can build up an immunity to them. The Bible list these three areas in 1 John 2:16. It refers to them "things of the world."

Worldly Way #1—"Cravings of Sinful Man." What in the world are cravings of sinful man?! Maybe "desires" or "pleasures" would be a more un-

76

derstandable word. This one deals with desire that you have because you are a person! They aren't bad by themselves, but the devil has come up with all kinds of ways to turn our natural desires into bad stuff. Make a list of all of the desires you can think of that people just naturally have: _____

_____

_____

_____

_____

_____

Now take a look at the desires you listed above. Which ones would you say we share with most animals? _____

_____

_____

If we don't learn to control our instinctual desires, we aren't any better off than cats or dogs. You've probably seen couples who reminded you of animals because they couldn't keep their paws off each other, even in public. How do you control these desires and not let them control you? Take a minute to discuss that question with the rest of the class. Don't be afraid to share your ideas. There isn't one special answer.

Now write down the answers to the question you discussed with the class that make the most sense to you. _____

_____

_____

_____

Since most of us find this area one of our weakest, we really have to watch ourselves. It helps to take inventory every now and then and take a look at our actions. Are your desires for food, sex, pleasure, or friendship controlling your actions or are YOU deciding your actions based on what God wants you to do? If you do things that you know are wrong to gain friends, then your desire for friendship is controlling you. If you abuse your body with food (too much or too little), then your desire for food has gotten out of whack. If you can't control yourself on dates and you find yourself daydreaming a lot about sex, then your desire for sex has you on a leash.

Don't let the devil get a hold on such potentially good things in your life and ruin the whole thing for you! You have to keep your eyes open at all times, because the devil is waiting for you to blink! Let's talk about the other areas of temptation and then we'll discuss some ways to resist temptation.

Wicked Way #2—"The Lust of His Eyes."—Have you ever watched little kids when a television commercial for a new toy comes on? The next time they go to the store, they just HAVE to have it! We all have a weakness in this area. Make a list of five things you have seen recently that you really want to have:

1. _____

2. _____

3. _____

4. _____

5. _____

The problems come when we find we can't rest until we have the things that our eyes see and we want them NOW! Married couples have problems when one partner lets his eyes wander and he wakes up to find that his looking around has aroused feelings of "having to have" another person. A great deal of stealing occurs because a person sees something he wants and he figures he can just take it. Our eyes can get us into a lot of trouble if we aren't careful! Read Matthew 5:29. What does it say to do with your eye if it causes you to sin? _____ That's pretty strong stuff!

It's easy to become proud when you've got lots of nice stuff.

Wicked Way #3—"The Boasting of What He Has and Does."—This part of 1 John 2:16 refers to pride. It's easy to become proud when you have lots of nice stuff. Have you ever found yourself looking down on a person because he doesn't have nice clothes or money? It's easy to fall into the trap of thinking we are something special. The devil even helps us out by giving us pointers in selfishness and pride. God wants us to feel good about ourselves, but He didn't intend for us to become preoccupied with our own importance.

How can I resist all of these temptations? What does Mark 14:38 say about it? _____

_____

_____

_____

You have to keep your eyes open and watch what you are doing. Here are four practical pointers on how to resist temptation.

1. Be aware of your weaknesses and try not to get into situations where you might be tempted in those areas.

2. Don't forget to pray. God will help you if you are sincere in wanting to overcome a temptation. Pray about it every day and let God guide you through or show you ways to escape.

3. Fill your time with good things. The less idle time you give the devil to play with, the better off you will be.

4. Keep your eyes open for an escape hatch. God won't let you be tempted beyond what you are able to resist. He makes that promise in 1 Corinthians

10:13. When you are tempted to do something you know you shouldn't do, start looking for the escape route. God has promised that it is there somewhere!

Just as hard times in your life can help you grow, overcoming temptation will make you a stronger person. Each time you resist makes the next resistance even easier. The key is to keep on trying to overcome. God will see that you come out a winner!

Keep trying to overcome and God will see that you come out a winner!

Group Activities

Have the following written on a large piece of butcher paper. Place it on the wall before the class:
1. Tempted to drink alcohol
2. Tempted to lust
3. Tempted to cheat

4. Tempted to gossip
5. Tempted to look at pornographic books and movies
6. Tempted to lie

Have the class play "Dear Abby." They will pretend that they are writing to help someone with each of these problems overcome their temptations. Have each person write a response to point out what the escape hatches might be in each of these situations. Encourage the class to be specific about what people can do to help avoid getting into the tempting situations again.

Discussion Questions

1. What is the best way to avoid being tempted?
2. Is it wrong if you are tempted to do bad things a lot?
3. Why does God let the devil tempt us so much?
4. What is the hardest thing about trying to avoid temptation?

11

LOOKING OUT
FOR . . . #2

Dear God,

  When I became a Christian, I thought I wouldn't
be selfish anymore. I still find myself wanting to
spend all of my time and all of my money on ME! I
always want to be first, and when I don't get to be, I
get angry. I want you in my life, but maybe I've
been wanting just enough of you to take away the
guilt I have about being so self-centered. Help me
learn to serve and to give to others. Show me how to
be a servant, Lord. I've heard it's even fun when you
really get into it!

David

Unfortunately, we live in a selfish world. Advertising is designed to make us look at ourselves and make ourselves happy. We are told we have to look out for Number 1, which, of course, is ME! I wonder if Paul knew about us when he wrote: "Do nothing out of selfish ambition or vain conceit, but in humility consider others better than yourselves" (Philip. 2:3, NIV).

Can you imagine enrolling in college and listing your major as "Servanthood"?

Me, a servant? Somehow, being a servant just doesn't sound like something you would want to grow up to be! Can you imagine enrolling in college and listing your major as "servanthood"? They would probably find you a padded desk! We don't have a very good impression of servants. We think of lowly people who have to follow orders, smell bad, are dumb, and don't have any money or clothes. So when God tells us that we are to become servants, we don't get real fired up. Look up Matthew 20:25–28. Write down why you think Jesus would have left heaven to come here and serve people whom He knew would kill Him. _____

_____

_____

_____

_____

These verses contain a word that's even worse than servant. SLAVE! Why would Jesus want His people to be slaves? _____

_____

_____

The answer is probably best stated in John 3:16. You probably know that verse well! God loved us so much that He was willing to let Jesus come and show us how to live and serve.

Choose me last! In the last part of Luke 9:35, Jesus says, "'If anyone wants to be first, he must be the very last, and the servant of all'" (NIV). Can you imagine two brothers jumping out of the car at a playground and running to the swings shouting, "Last! I get last swing!". That's not usually the way it happens! To be the servant that Jesus wants us to be, we have to revise our thinking. The first step is to start putting other people first and yourself last. List several things you could do this week to put others before yourself. Try to think of specific things that you can plan on trying this week:

_____

_____

_____

_____

_____

The next step involves the last part of the verse we just read, the part about being the servant of all. Just who are we supposed to serve? We can't possibly serve everyone in the world, so what is God talking about? _____

_____

_____

_____

God wants us to keep our eyes open for people who NEED us. That means we should try to notice when people look like they are having a rough day, when work needs to be done around the house, when the older people in your neighborhood need help with yardwork, when you see someone fall and get hurt, or when anyone else has a need that we are able to help with. Write down the names of several people whom you might be able to serve this week in some special way:

Serve #1: _____

Serve #2: _____

Serve #3: _____

Sometimes serving is as simple as listening to someone with a problem. But in other situations you might get into something that takes all of your free time. Praying for someone's needs is a good way to serve. One big way to serve others is to tell them about Jesus. It's scary to think that the lady whose yard we mow free might ask us on the judgment day why we mowed her yard every week and never told her what she needed to know to be saved. Putting yourself last helps you put everything in perspective. You will probably notice a difference in the way people respond to you. They will enjoy being around you because you treat them so well!

Would your mom pass out if you did the dishes without being told?

Where do I start? A good place to start would be with your family at home. Try to surprise your parents by secretly doing some housework. Would your mom pass out if you did the dishes without being asked to? Look for ways to do things for your family without them knowing it was you. It can really be lots of fun to see them trying to figure out who did it! After you have started serving your family, move out to your friends. From there, the world is the limit! If you put your mind to it, you can find all kinds of ways to serve people.

Service Menu. Make a list of ways that you could serve the people around you:

1. _____
2. _____
3. _____
4. _____
5. _____
6. _____
7. _____
8. _____

Now go back to your list and write down a name beside each way to serve. That will be your project for the week. Try to serve the people on your list without their knowing who is doing it. Next week come back and see how many of them you were able to keep it from! There are millions of fun ways you can serve people! Don't buy into the poor image that servants have. You can serve by listening to someone, by helping friends deal with problems, helping around the house, watching your little brother or sister for your parents—and the list goes on and on! Read 1 Corinthians 15:58. That's even added incentive to serve. God isn't going to let your hard work go to waste. Even if the people you do things for don't notice, God is keeping tabs, and He will reward you!

The next time you find yourself in a situation where you have a chance to serve, jump in with both feet. Get involved with people! God may have placed you in that situation because He knew that He could share His love with them through YOU! Start working now to improve your serve. Develop the attitudes that Christ wants you to have as His special servant on earth.

Group Activity

Spend your activity time today trying to change the boring image that servanthood has. Brainstorm creative and fun ways that your class could serve others. Start out by having each person tell about one time when they did something neat for someone anonymously. Then challenge yourselves to come up with one special project that you could do as a class. One youth group went driving around on a hot summer day with a cooler of cold cokes. Attached to the cokes was a poster that said, "A cup of cold water (coke) in His name" (Mark 9:41). They searched for working people who looked hot and thirsty. The looks they got as they hopped out of the van and delivered the cokes were hilarious, but there were a lot of happy workmen around town that day! Serving people isn't boring unless YOU make it that way! See what your group can come up with!

12

IT RUNS IN THE FAMILY

Dear Lord,

I'm so lonely. How is it possible to be in such a big school and feel all alone? There must be something wrong with me. Not many people seem to like me very much. I try not to do some of the bad things they do, like drinking and fooling around on dates, so they all think I'm a weirdo or something. I really need a friend now, Lord. I just can't seem to find anyone who likes me just like I am and who will help me be a stronger Christian instead of pulling me away. Please help me find a friend like that!

John

Have you ever felt like you were all alone?

Have you ever felt as if you were all alone? Probably all of us have felt that way at times. If you are really trying to be a Christian at school, you have probably felt that way a lot. It isn't easy to deal with those lonely feelings, because we all want to be loved and accepted. What advice would you give John about the problems he describes in his prayer?

Just keep trying to be a Christian. you're not the wierdo for trying to follow God. There the wierdos for drinking and being idiots.

What do you think of when you hear the word "fellowship"? *God, Church, people Christians, food*

We usually hear the word used to describe a meal
that we have after services. Fellowship is one of the
keys to surviving life as a Christian. Fellowship is
any time that Christians are together having fun,
studying the Bible or praying, talking, or encouraging each other in any way. If you are a Christian,
you have a new family to whom you belong. You are
responsible for encouraging the others in your family, just like they are responsible for helping you
grow and stay excited about being a Christian.
Make a list of five things that your family at home
(parents, brothers, and sisters) does for you:

1. ~~Make my meals~~
2. ~~Take me to Church~~
3. ~~Take me to school~~
4. ~~Take care of me~~ Keep me sa
5. ~~Give me a house~~ fe

Now try to think of five things that church fam-
ilies should try to do for one another:

1. Let's people come and worship
2. Give money
3. Help the sick
4. Prepare meals
5. Love one another

Let's take a deeper look at this thing called fellowship. It's an important part of our lives, because
most of us couldn't make it alone. We really need
each other! Look up Psalm 1:1–2. What three

things does God say you should avoid if you want to be happy (blessed)? *Don't stand in the way of sinners, walk with ungodly, sit in way of scornful!*

Now that we know three things we shouldn't do, what do you think is the main reason Christians need to hang around other Christians? *to encourage each other to do the right things*

Encouragement is a good word to describe what spending time with other Christians is all about. If you have ever had to stand up for your Christian beliefs all alone, you know what a tough job that can be. If there are several Christians with you, it isn't as hard. It gets really difficult to behave like a Christian when all of your friends aren't Christians. Maybe you don't know of any other Christians in your school. Then, it's YOUR job to bring some of the other people there to Christ! Maybe that wouldn't be thought of as cool, but that is what God wants you to do (Mark 16:15). Just because you are the only Christian in a group doesn't give you an excuse to back down and let the others run the show. If you stand up, there will probably be others who will start to stand up with you. Fellowship is important, because it can give us the strength to do daring things like that!

What does God say? Look up the following verses and try to find at least one reason from each verse why Christians need fellowship.

Proverbs 27:17 _We need to sharpen one another_

Psalm 133:1 _It's ~~un~~pleasant to dwell in unity_

Hebrews 10:24 _Let's encourage people to do good_

Proverbs 13:20 _Walk and do good with Christians_

Who's in/who's out? Good Christian fellowship should involve all of the Christians who want to be a part of the group. Most groups tend to let in only those people whom they like or who have similar interests. You have probably seen that happen in your youth group or at school. If you have ever been the one who is left out, you know how much it can hurt. We need to make an effort to encourage everyone, not just the people we like or who like us. List the names of three people whom you need to get to know and to encourage:

We need to make an effort to encourage everyone.

94

1. _____

2. _____

3. _____

Lots of people hang around with the drug group at school because they often do a better job of accepting people into their groups than Christians do. That's sad! Work at breaking up any cliques you are a part of, and start reaching out to other people. It will be hard to explain to God why the other Christians at your school wound up in the drug group because they weren't accepted by your group.

How to be a Christian friend. Make a list of qualities that you look for when you are looking for friends: _____

_____

_____

_____

_____

_____

How many of these qualities do you have? The key to being a Christian friend is being a friend yourself. If you reach out and try to be a friend, you'll have lots of friends in return! People can't resist hanging around someone who builds them up and cares about them. Write a prayer asking God to help you draw more people into your Christian fellowship and make it your goal this week to reach out and pull people into your group!

DEAR GOD, _____

_____

_____
_____
_____
_____
_____
_____
_____
_____

Group Activities

Play a game called "Can of Worms." The worms are questions that make you squirm. Before the class the teacher should write these questions on small pieces of paper and place them in a can. Pick one person to start the session. That person draws a question, reads it aloud, and gives his answer. He then discards the question and the next person takes his turn. You should have one question per person. Break down into smaller groups and have several sets of questions if you have a large group. Here are some "worms" you can use.

1. Why do you think it is important for a Christian to date other Christians or why do you think it doesn't matter?

2. What qualities should a person look for in a friend?

3. Do you feel like you have more close friends at school or at church? Why do you feel that way?

4. List five things that you and your friends often talk about.

5. Is it O.K. for a Christian to go to wild parties as long as he/she doesn't participate?

6. Why is it important to be a friend if you want to make friends?

7. What advice would Jesus give you about your friends?

13

A FRIEND IN NEED

Friends are some of the most important people in our lives. They're the people we most often go to when we need advice, when we want to borrow something, or when we just want to relax and have a good time. Take just a second and make a list of your best friends, the ones you are closest to.

_____

_____

_____

_____

_____

If these people needed food, would you share yours with them? If they needed clothes, would you let them borrow yours? Most of us have a friend or two that we would do anything for. Too often, we leave out the most important thing we could do for a friend in need. Why do you think so many Christians are afraid to tell their friends about Jesus? List the main reasons you think of in the stumbling blocks in the path below.

A lot of times, people give reasons like these:

- I'm scared.
- I don't know what to say.

Why are so many Christians afraid to tell their friends about Jesus?

- I don't want to offend them.
- What if they think I'm a nerd?

Sometimes it helps to think about your friends as really having a need for Jesus. So many people mess up their lives because they don't know Jesus. You have to realize that you have the answers to your friends' needs! That puts a responsibility on your shoulders. But more than that, it gives you the exciting opportunity to fill a very special blank spot in your friends' lives. Go back to your list of friends at the beginning of this lesson. Put a star by the names of those who aren't Christians. That's where you will start!

If you notice, Jesus started his ministry with twelve people with whom He developed a very special relationship. You start with your closest friends, too. If all of your closest friends are Chris-

99

tians, make another list of names of people you know who aren't Christians. Now that you have your list of names, what do you think Jesus would do to reach out to these special people? What approach would He take to help them see the light? Take a look at the following scriptures and see if you can pick out what Jesus did to reach out to the people involved.

John 4:1–26: _____

_____

_____

Mark 6:30–44: _____

_____

_____

Luke 5:17–26: _____

_____

Jesus almost always did what He could to meet people's physical needs before he taught them. That is a valuable lesson for us to consider. A lot of your friends have problems at home, problems in school, self-esteem problems, or any number of other problems all jumbled up in their lives. You can really be of help to these people. Often we have a tendency to say, "There's nothing I can do" when we hear about a friend with an alcoholic parent or some other big problem. What do you think Jesus would do to teach a person who:

- Had a parent who abused him?
- Was failing in school?
- Had a drug or alcohol problem?

There's Nothing I can Do!

• Didn't like himself?

There are all kinds of things you can do to reach out to your friends. Take another look at your list of friends. Make notes beside their names if you can think of a specific problem you could help them with. Then try to come up with one idea of a way that you could reach out to that friend in a special way. The way to begin sharing Jesus is by learning how He loved people. Once you get into the habit of giving yourself to others, telling them about Jesus becomes a more natural response.

So What Do I Do Now? Make the decision to try to meet your friends' needs. That will get you started in the right direction. Then, make sure you are working to grow closer to God yourself. Pray every day for the physical and spiritual needs of your friends. When your friends see what a caring person you are and how you are really interested in their problems and in helping them, you'll begin to see a difference in them. People have a hard time holding back when they come in contact with Jesus' love. And that's what you will be spreading—Jesus' love!

Finally, you can begin to share with them that you pray for them and that God has begun to make a difference in your life. Don't hold back when you have the answers to the questions in your friends' lives. Look at it as your privilege to bring Jesus into the lives of the special people around you!

Group Activity

Have the group pair off and play the "why" game. The partners should sit facing each other. One person should begin by telling about his faith and beliefs in God. To each of his/her statements, the other person should ask "why?". Have them go on and try to explain their faith as well as they can. Then have the partners switch roles. After you do this activity, talk about the things that make us most uncomfortable about sharing Jesus with others. Help the students see what a difference it would make if someone who had really shown love and compassion for you told you about Jesus as opposed to someone you didn't know or who had been unkind to you. Encourage each person to pick out a person to reach out to during the coming week. You might even follow up next week by having everyone talk about what they did.

Group Discussion

Talk about what teenagers can do to reach out to people and to teach them about Jesus by the way they love others. Have your group list some problems that are common among their friends. Then let the whole group search for ways to reach out to people with those kinds of problems.

God - an invisible, mighty, perfect, creator of Earth and every living thing who loves us an forgives our Sins

Printed in the United States
118139LV00002B/1-18/A

9 780892 253128